LIKE

Seven Rules and 10 Simple Steps for Social Media in Your Campaign (in Politics, Business or Otherwise)

LIKE

Seven Rules and 10 Simple Steps for Social Media in Your Campaign (in Politics, Business or Otherwise)

By Kelly Groehler
with Dave Ladd, Greg Swanholm, and
Bass Zanjani

ISBN 978-1-105-40142-8

Table of Contents

Table of Contents

Foreword
Why LIKE can help any campaign

Before we start, take a minute to examine your own feelings on the subject at hand: social media.

Is social media something you choose to ignore? Do you pray that it's some passing fad? Do you scoff at invitations to join Facebook, because an actual friend is better than a virtual one? Do you wonder aloud if a tweet and a twit are the same thing? And when forced to deal with social media, do you automatically turn to your youngest staffer (or worse, your own children) and expect them to handle it, because you have neither the time or interest?

If you said yes to one or more of these questions, then this book is for you.

The premise of LIKE is simple: follow the rules, and take the right steps to use social media in any campaign — or to deliver any message.

Here's why: Hundreds of millions of individuals today, around the world, have the power of choice – and a voice – more than at any point in the history of humankind. Young or old, urban or rural, in nearly every economic class, we have online access like never before, with more ways than ever to connect: a computer, a mobile phone, a smart phone, even a television or an automobile. We can — and do — share everything, from anywhere, and everywhere, whenever we want.

At the time of publication, people do the following every 60 seconds (source: Go-Globe.com):

- Run nearly 700,000 Google searches

- Post more than 695,000 status updates to Facebook

- Post 12,000 new ads to Craigslist

- Post 600+ new videos (25 hours of content) to YouTube

- Tweet 98,000+ updates through Twitter

- Create more than 100 LinkedIn accounts

But the key question is: what do all of these numbers actually mean?

Numbers of this size are intimidating — and easy to misunderstand. However, they are merely incidental, showing how fast the information is moving, or the number of eyeballs following social media at any given point in time. They're outputs. Trying to grasp them can be overwhelming and paralyze smart thinking as to the true nature of social media, and how to engage society through their diverse menu of channels.

Instead, try looking at the numbers this way:

Every 60 seconds, millions of individuals are telling each other what they like, and what they dislike.

- They are searching for answers on Google

- They are sharing information with friends on Facebook

- They are trading goods and services on Craigslist

- They are creating and watching videos on YouTube

- They are telling their Twitter followers what they think

- They are networking and seeking job opportunities through LinkedIn

Like. Dislike. The key to understanding social media is to focus not on the volume or speed of the information, but rather how these expressions are shared so willingly via social media channels — and how you, in turn, can navigate your own campaign and communications strategy through the "likes" and "dislikes."

The seven rules of LIKE, and the 10 steps outlined in this book, are well suited for the individual running for elected office — whether that office is the local school board or the United States Senate. The rules and steps are intentionally simple, to help those with a more novice sense of social media to grasp why these channels are critical in today's campaign cycles, and how to get into the habit of using them effectively and efficiently.

X

But while an election campaign is the illustration, this is not a guide solely for those seeking public office. These rules and steps have universal appeal and are applicable to virtually any cause, campaign, or effort that is seeking help to get on board with social media: Nonprofit cause, grassroots campaign, academic outreach, fundraising, community organizing — it can even help a business focus its online activity.

Moving forward, the seven rules of LIKE are essential for everything we do. When the number of active social media users worldwide exceeds the total populations of several countries, it's probably time to stop wishing it will go away.

The way we have conversations with constituents has permanently shifted, thanks to the tools and channels of social media. Whether we want to lead in our communities, fix our country, or solve the world's problems, it is imperative that we are mindful of relationships and conversations with those we are trying to engage. We can no longer assume that citizens — or customers, for that matter — will just take our word for it. They have their own opinions, and buying into your campaign promise, or your organization's message, is entirely optional.

Ultimately, they will choose whether to "like" what you stand for, and whether you will win.

So let's get started.

"There are certain core values that we believe in as Americans that we believe are universal: freedom of speech, freedom of expression... people being able to use social networking or any other mechanisms to communicate with each other and to express their concerns."

President Barack Obama, Jan. 28, 2011

Chapter I
Why LIKE is no longer optional for a campaign

Consider this scenario:

You're up for election, and your opponent has a strong pro-family agenda. You attend a weekend community parade to campaign - but instead of riding on a float, you walk the route, greeting the crowds and shaking hands. A parent holds out his baby for a photo. You take the child and smile for the camera. The baby starts crying, and you twist your face at the smell of a dirty diaper. Someone in the crowd captures the moment with a smart phone photo, and posts it within seconds to Twitter, with a caption: "proof this candidate doesn't like kids." Within fifteen minutes, the photo has been viewed and shared by thousands of other constituents. Within thirty minutes, the TV stations are calling your staff for comment.

One might argue that this presents a worst-case scenario, or that it's an incredibly slow news day if the assignment desks are calling for comment. But this is not a far-fetched possibility with social media. Both your supporters and detractors are well equipped with smart phones to create their own content and share their interpretations of it — both good and bad. If anything, it creates a time drain for you and your staff, who now have to spend time defending your facial expressions.

More broadly, the intersection of social media activity with civic life is very real. A survey in October 2011 by digital agency Digitas found that 88 percent of registered voters in the United States are active users of social media. Furthermore, in January 2011, the Pew Internet & American Life Project found that more than 25 percent of Americans used the Internet as a major source of campaign news in 2010, up from 7 percent in 2002.

In other words, the same people sharing millions of "likes" and "dislikes" every sixty seconds through social media are the same people who can make or break your election or create reputation risks for your organization.

This reality is antithetical to traditional campaign communications strategies, where messages and promises often rely on polling, focus groups, and surveys before they're delivered. Because social media is a spontaneous conversation, the dialogue takes place on the terms of the voters who very likely want to engage with you in an immediate, rapid-fire manner. Rarely is there any time under these circumstances to vet every single response.

While this reality presents a serious wake-up call, any campaign can (and should) rise to meet the challenge. The traditional campaign tools, such as advertising, polling, door knocking, fundraisers, speeches, debates, earned media coverage and websites, are critical, and will continue to have relevance.

But given the fact that citizens can influence a campaign like never before, the additional use of specific social media tools to engage with them is a minimum requirement. And it's critical to understand the unique trait of these tools: they are channels for *conversation*, more than information.

Campaigns have traditionally relied on marketing a candidate as someone who defined the problem and the solution, then worked to persuade voters that it was the right problem and solution to care about. Today, people aren't waiting for one person to figure it out. Social media is used widely — in business and in communities — to build consensus around the definition of a problem, and then "crowd-source" the solution (asking those who helped define the problem for their ideas to fix it). So as fewer put their faith in one leader who knows everything to one who can be a "voice of understanding and reason" and shepherd others to fix a problem, the candidate marketed as a singular "voice of authority" is quickly becoming a position with diminishing returns.

Think of it this way: if citizens are empowered in their daily lives to choose who to follow, search for what they need, buy whatever they want, and share their "likes" and "dislikes" with those who follow them in social networks, what incentive do they have to engage with your campaign purely through the traditional tools? And if they don't endorse your platform or agenda, what prevents them from sharing their "dislike" with others?

The detractor witnessing your dirty-diaper grimace didn't verbally shout to the parade crowd that you don't like kids; he shouted it out to an even larger and noisy crowd online. So should you stop shaking hands and kissing babies? Absolutely not. But shaking hands and kissing babies will no longer be enough to earn more "likes" for your campaign.

The voice of the citizen through social media cannot be turned off. Instead, that voice needs to know that you're listening — and that you're intentionally participating in the conversations.

And all of the other, more traditional campaign tools will need to adjust to this new reality.

Chapter 2

DISLIKE: Why campaign strategies need to adapt

"All elections are a choice... positive/negative/contrast campaigns in terms of tone and style." Jeff Blodgett, Wellstone Action, December 2010

"Dislikes" reveal themselves through social media in a variety of ways. On the streaming music site Pandora.com, a listener can click a thumbs-up icon to "like" a song, or a thumbs-down icon to "dislike" it. Friends and followers can complain, argue, and debate with one another, with each of their follower lists following the conversation. Detractors can snap unflattering photos on a smart phone and pass them around, quickly and widely, with unfair or untrue captions. And sometimes, a "dislike" can be expressed as simply not talking about an issue – or identifying oneself as undecided.

Now think about those **88** percent of registered voters in the United States who are active social media users. What would happen if those voters decide to actively dislike your campaign? Or, if they remain undecided because they think you're not engaging them? They might think you don't represent them, and their "dislike" could reveal itself at the voting booth.

The **88** percent has been a growing percentage of the population for several years; what is evident is the need for strategies to adapt to this majority and engage the citizen voice. As an example, let's look to one race, in one state, during the 2010 U.S. midterm elections.

Minnesota consistently leads the United States during elections with the highest turnout of eligible voters: According to the U.S. Election Project, Minnesota led the country in turnout in 2004, with 77 percent of eligible voters turning out compared to 60 percent in the nation as a whole. And during the 2010 mid-term elections, Minnesota saw 55.9 percent of eligible voters participating, compared to 41.6 percent turnout for the nation as a whole.

It's also a state with a legacy of progressive, strategic thinking when it comes to development of public policy and citizen engagement that widely represents the political spectrum — from radical to fundamental, liberal to conservative, independent to party-endorsed.

Wellstone Action, a think tank named for the late United States Senator Paul Wellstone, is one example of this legacy. The group's model for approaching campaigns and policy-making is thoughtful, strategic, and has stood the test of time:

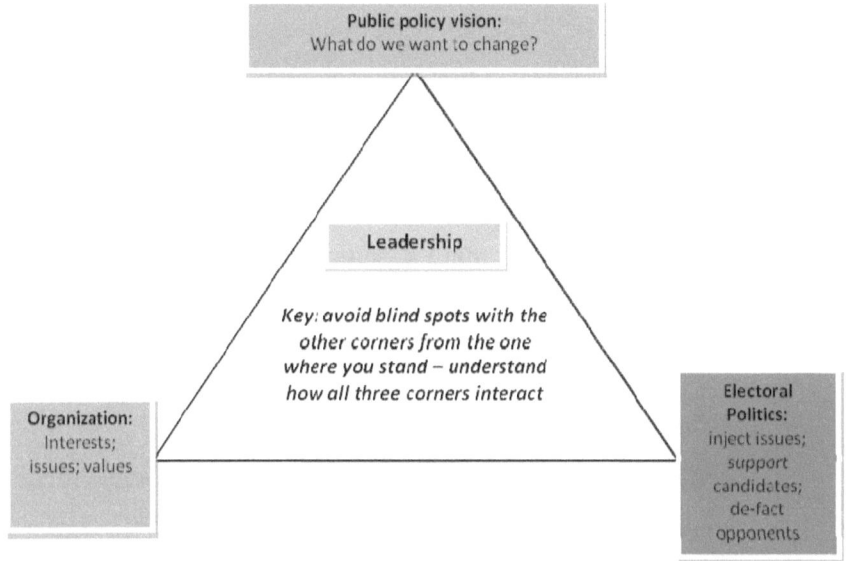

MODEL: Policy Leadership Pyramid (Source: Wellstone Action, 2010)

It's fair to say that some version of this model was put to good use by the vast majority of 2010 midterm campaigns. At the same time, the vast majority of U.S. voters were actively using social media, and one in four turned to the Web as the major source of midterm campaign news.

But in general, the 2010 midterm campaigns chose to execute the model, and influence voters, through more traditional means of communications like advertising, news coverage, and grassroots outreach. And while elections still took place, and there were winners and losers, the general manner campaigns chose to communicate revealed a noticeable gap in connecting with voters through social media. In some cases, the races also demonstrated that some of those traditional tools are not as effective in winning elections, or delivering a message, as they once were.

In Minnesota, a three-way gubernatorial race with no incumbent played out in just this way:

- The winner, Mark Dayton (D), focused his campaign primarily on the state's senior demographic, and thus opted not to feature any substantial social media integration. (Worth noting: The Pew Internet & American Life Project found only 20 percent of U.S. internet users, ages 50-64, was using social media networking sites in 2010 on a daily basis. By August 2011, well after this race, daily use among the same age group had grown to 65 percent.)

- The campaign for Tom Emmer (R) integrated social media strategies far greater and with more consistency than the other two gubernatorial candidates. However, Emmer was embattled by detractors who effectively utilized social media to call into question his positions on issues.

- Although Tom Horner (I) worked to intersect earned and paid media with social media, his campaign lacked a strong base of social media-based Independents and other "surrogates" to carry his messages against the state's traditional two-party strength. That said, Horner captured a traditional campaign coup, securing all but one editorial endorsement from the state's daily newspapers. In the end, though, he secured only 12 percent of the vote.

Among the three candidates' circles of influence, the total percentage of social media followers and deliberate online content from major donors and political parties were low in 2010, with nascent to non-existent use of social media for fundraising. The most notable users were mainstream media, who leveraged social media to move news and information to their followers.

It's important to underscore that the 2010 Minnesota gubernatorial race was not decided on social media use. Rather, the campaigns took place at a time when the potential and influence of the voice of the citizen online was not yet widely recognized nor understood. Mr. Horner, for instance, says that if he were to start over again, social media would be the first consideration for his campaign communications strategy — with the traditional tools adjusted to supplement social media platforms.

As more candidates and campaigns realize that the majority of voters actively use social media, the opportunity to revisit the idea of the traditional policy leadership model presents itself. While the principles are largely the same, the three corners of the pyramid aren't as rigid. If voters aren't waiting for a voice of authority to tell them what to do, but are instead expressing their own ideas and solutions, then the model starts to bend. This also means that leadership is no longer the idea of one elected official, or one party, in the center, anticipating blind spots from the corners.

Instead, a more progressive engagement of all constituents, and communications channels, is required to engage the citizen voice. And smart use of social media in campaigns makes it possible.

MODEL 2: Policy Leadership & Citizen Engagement Model

Chapter 3

The seven rules of LIKE: Social media as a critical campaign tool

"Like." "Dislike." The key to successful integration of social media into any campaign is to focus on these two expressions — not the rate by which the information moves, or how many social media channels exist. Done well, it can help an unknown candidate build a base, or help a campaign compete with a well-funded opponent.

One might be tempted to leap forward and start following the 10 steps in the next chapter. But doing so misses the whole point of LIKE. While ignoring social media is no longer an option, ignoring the rules by which social media really works is a recipe for disaster.

The idea of LIKE has seven simple rules. Once you read them, you'll likely conclude that you knew them all along. But starting with the rules in mind is always the best approach, especially when you're working to earn the "likes" of others.

Rule 1: A campaign strategy without social media isn't 100 percent complete.

A common misperception of social media is that it's optional. More dangerous is an assumption that it's free. Given the fact that these channels are literally "on" every second, taking an episodic or occasional approach will not work. Their best use will require resources to implement, manage, and monitor them based on the individual platform's strengths and weaknesses.

Developing message discipline in social media is no different than in regular media, despite the speed at which the conversations take place. Said another way, social media does not displace a good strategy or a strong message platform. Make sure you have both of those first, and apply them to the social media channels. And your communications manager must know how they work and how to manage them in concert with all other activities and traditional tools.

Rule 2: Think about your personal brand, because it will be tested like never before.

Humanizing a campaign is more important than ever. Social media can help voters and consumers view you as an accessible candidate or worthy organization who understands their priorities, and provides the means for them to engage directly with your campaign or stated mission — with minimal effort or deployment of your own resources. The potential for leverage in fundraising and endorsements is high, whether you manage your own social media participation, your staff leverages your name on your behalf, or both. But keep in mind:

people will expect to hear your personal voice, to see your human side, good and bad, and to believe that you have a clear stance on issues. Make sure you manage to those expectations.

Rule 3: The greatest influence on a vote is the opinion of someone the voter trusts.

This is the core essence of "like" — and "dislike." More than ever, trust is critical to winning. And while the online citizen voice is not fully displacing the power of major funders or political parties, it will never go away. Pay attention to how you navigate relationships with your stakeholder groups, and make sure they're consistent with your online conversations. And understand that — thanks to technology — what you say to anyone, anywhere, and at any time, is a public statement. Any attempt to control or forge "likes" or "dislikes" for your message has a high probability of backfiring. Integrity, trust and character are just as important for your campaign, whether engaging the voter or consumer online or shaking hands at a parade.

Rule 4: Know thy audiences and how to best engage them online.

Get to know the voters and constituents most important to your campaign's success, and use that knowledge to guide how and when you engage them. Pay attention to how they use social media and how they engage with one another, and what they expect (or don't expect) from your campaign. Keep in mind that local and hyper-local messaging is just as important online as it is when using traditional communications channels. Campaigns can reach voters beyond major media markets in specific geographic areas for conversations, so make sure your social media messages are as local (and relevant to your followers) as possible. And don't forget: Younger generations are marching on the web, and they defy you to connect with them. They have more power than ever, so go meet them online and start the conversation.

Rule 5: Traditional media and social media are always — always — interconnected.

Mainstream media relies on social media more than ever for fact checking, identifying sources for their own stories, and extending the reach of their own news coverage. Reporters and pundits are highly influential and tend to have higher numbers of followers than others. Pay attention to the intersections of their news with social outreach, and think of ways to maximize earned/mainstream media and social media for your own strategies.

Additionally, social media can be a predictive tool for mainstream coverage. It's a tremendous way to gauge reaction to a position, a news story, or a moment in time because followers will "like" or "dislike" the news. Social media allows you to see that exchange.

Rule 6: The best defense is a strong offense.

Human beings have a long history of first weaponizing tools before using them for good. While President Barack Obama's 2008 win is held up as the model for excellent utilization of social media, more generally social media to date has commonly been weaponized by political campaigns. One common use is to influence greater media attention through trench warfare — right or wrong, it can generate "gotcha moments" that turn faux into reality. (Remember the parade scenario? Your grimace has turned into the lead for the 6 p.m. news.) Resist the urge to weaponize them, yourself, but be ready for your opponents to utilize social media as attack tools. Consider ways to deflate their power by building and strengthening your own personal brand with voters, media, and influencers (both online and offline).

Rule 7: Manage social media. Every. Single. Day.

It's critical that candidates and their respective campaigns dedicate professional staff resources to effectively utilize social media platforms within their communications operation. An overall plan should be drafted at the beginning of the campaign, with social media following the same message discipline that is utilized in all other communications tools. Because social media expects content, think of how earned media (news coverage), paid media (advertising and related video), and owned media (constituent videos, live events, speeches, etc.) is fed and spread throughout the campaign's social media channels. Invest in dedicated, daily management and monitoring, plus staffers or advisers who keep pace with the various channels and how they're constantly changing.

And don't forget: use of social media builds a base for governing. Those who "like" you enough to vote you into office expect you'll keep in touch, and use the channels to build consensus around direction and policy choices. Once you start, you'll need to remain engaged.

Chapter 4
The 10 steps: A basic social media planning template

Now that you've had a chance to read the rules, it's time to put them into practice. The following 10 steps are fundamental ways to move from worrying about — or ignoring — social media, to actually using it to your advantage.

Step 1: Assess your current situation.

It might seem obvious, but some of the best plans have clear outcomes that everyone understands and follows. Businesses fail and campaigns are lost when there isn't a common understanding of the end goal or a definition of success. Take the time to self-assess, with your campaign team and advisers, the current state of your candidacy. Outline your goals — for election, fundraising, key endorsements, stakeholders, media contacts, and constituent base. Write them down, and make sure your entire staff understands and endorses them.

Step 2: Intentionally set objectives, so you know how success is to be measured later.

All communications — including social media — must be a "toward what end" proposition: the "likes" that drive to the bigger goals outlined above. Work with your chief of staff and communications director to clearly spell out the reputation and communications objectives you want to achieve.

Step 3: Take inventory of your entire campaign communications ecosystem and budget.

Review all campaign and candidate outreach and communications channels, including paid (e.g., advertising), earned (e.g., traditional media coverage), events (fundraisers, debates, etc.), and owned (websites, blogs, and social media assets that are controlled and managed by the candidate or the campaign). Know what you have, how current the content is within each, how often it's updated, and how much you're spending on communications activities:

1. Campaign website, blog, etc.

2. Prior campaign collateral/content/materials, if any

3. Public events/forums — date, time, recap of prior events, results, etc.

4. Campaign staff training/meetings — agendas, materials, etc.

5. Existing polling, related reports — own campaign, other candidates, etc.

6. Any candidate or staff research/writing/publications/books/blogs/sites

7. Media coverage — noted reporter relationships, tone and share of voice of coverage, etc.

8. Any affiliation, partners, funders – own sites, social media channels, etc.

Step 4: Recognize your existing social media strengths and assets.

Determine the social media assets your campaign already has in place — campaign owned, and candidate owned. Also understand the social media fluency among your staff. Revisit the social media statistics already culled by the staff and the candidate. Look at your websites; are visitors able to easily share posts and content with their own followers (with buttons to "like" or "click to share")? Where are the most noted placements and citations from the candidate's social media/online stream by mainstream and online sources? How is content repurposed and reverberated by others through third party social media channels (such as tweets by reporters or viewers)? Have a clear idea of your current presence and influence in social media channels. Later, you'll need to cross check with the social media use patterns of your constituents.

Step 5: Staff up and allocate resources.

Make sure staff resources are in place to manage social media as deliberately as any other earned, paid or owned channel. Ensure budget dollars are allocated for content development that can be shared across paid, earned, owned, and social channels, and have designated staff to help manage the flow.

Your communications staff should be well-versed in current social media channels and tools. Hold them accountable to staying current on campaign rules as they apply to social media, and entrust them to provide training for all staff.

Since your staff is likely to utilize social media in their personal lives, provide guidelines for how they are expected to represent the campaign through their own activities. There are a number of publicly-available social media policies and guidelines that can serve as a template for your campaign's own guidelines.

Step 6: Know thy audiences.

Auditing the current social media activity of those who are of greatest influence to your campaign: know who is influential and active via social media circles today, and how (if at all) they current follow you or your campaign.

Audience audit.

If time and resources allow, audit the audiences across all party and candidate programming and channels — including, but not limited to voters, funders, political action committees (PACs), party leadership, and key political reporters. If possible, understand their own spheres of influence beyond their own engagement with the party or the candidate. Determine the type, frequency, and patterns of use of social media by audience segments, themselves. This is worth the investment to pinpoint how they intersect with the party, the candidate, and the issues that matter most to the election at hand.

Party and campaign social media audit.

Revisit the inventory of all online and social media channels and activity within the whole of the political party, and the campaign itself — how they're used, how frequently, and who manages them. Include Facebook pages, Google+ accounts, Twitter handles, Flickr accounts, YouTube channels, and blogs. Create an index of individual social media users within the party, including frequency of use and number of followers. Last, but not least, determine how measurement is handled, if at all, to gauge impact and influence through social media.

Competitive audit.

Outline and track activity of the other parties and candidates, as well as their own circles of influence. Which blogs, individuals, or groups — formal or informal — are competing for the audience mindshare that your campaign seeks? What are their social media patterns? Are there any impersonators using your name (for example, a fake Twitter account)?

Event audit.

Map out and regularly update the calendar for your programming and events (including mailers, debates and appearances) for the next year. Target natural points of intersections where a moment in time can be created to connect with supporters and voters via social media, with each event as the backdrop. For example, can you create a live event on your website, and ask your followers to share the link with their followers?

Media audit.

Map out and regularly update the media who most closely follow you or your organization, your campaign, and the race. Determine how their editorial content intersects with social media channels, how they stand independent of their news outlets, and how they engage with your competition.

Campaign advertising audit.

How much is budgeted for commercial development and ad buys, and how do the viewership numbers and reach compare to earned and social media channels? This is a key step to balance out total campaign communication spend, and ensure dollars are set aside to engage constituents across multiple channels.

Step 7: Build social media tools directly into your overall campaign communications activity.

Your communications staff should be equipped to prioritize and budget the following, once the audit findings clearly show areas of opportunity for your campaign.

Upgrade functionality of current candidate and campaign online sites, blogs, etc.

Maximize current social media integrations within the current online experience, mainly your campaign's website. Plan for regular updates with fresh posts and content; add sharing links where possible, so it's easy for viewers to share what they see on your website with their own social networks. Explore various basic and premium tools that can integrate with your site and enrich the experience — for example, stream live debates from your page for your followers, or host live chats with the campaign.

Expand your campaign's brand and presence in other social media channels.

Acquire all URLs, handles, and hashtags available for the candidate, campaign or organization (some are free, others might require an investment). Ensure the campaign has a portfolio of social media channels and presence: a Twitter account and Facebook page are the current basics. Invite followers to like, subscribe, even donate. Instantly post content on the page from the candidate website and other sources, and guide others to people and pages worth following. And make sure all of your current supporters are aware that you now have these social media accounts, so they can opt in to follow you and recommend to their own followers.

Upgrade your content.

Online content – blog posts, news releases, even videos – are quickly outdated. Daily or weekly video blog posts, infographics, recurring features, and webinars with online chat integrations are all ways to improve the interaction and engagement through the site. Additionally, ensure distribution of latest posts and updates with existing relevant "hashtag" conversations (for example, #mnleg is commonly used for tweets related to state government in Minnesota). The tools available today to record and post a video, or stream an event, are low cost and simple to use.

Use your own online sites, content, and presence to engage other audiences in the political party ecosystem.

Identify ways to ensure your campaign communications efforts, including social media content, is integrated with your endorsing party's own online and social activity, in particular when the content reflects the mission of the campaign. Host live streaming events of other party activity for viewing on the campaign site and channels, and offer to host party chats via the candidate's social media channels (including, but not limited to, debates, guest speakers, and annual events). Fully integrate social media tools through the party channels to deliver the content and engage conversations about the events and programming.

Build social media into every campaign moment in time.

If you're participating in a debate, your staff should post live updates and reports. Consider streaming the debate on your site to expand the viewership, particularly for those constituents beyond traditional media markets. Find other ways to fold social media into every campaign moment in time, to keep your followers informed.

Step 8: Identify your existing social media influencers, and how to deepen your connections

You might not realize it, but you have supporters who are savvy with social media. Understand who is influential and active, and elicit their help to make your own connections.

Take an inside-out approach to expand engagement with the campaign via social media

Target those with vested interest in the campaign — but who perhaps might not be currently engaged with your website or social media pages — to initially grow your base. Ask about their own social media preferences, and ask them to invite others to check out your online presence. Welcome their feedback, even if negative or constructive. You might find simple ways to improve your online presence, and make it better for your followers.

Leverage media partnerships.

Maximize any existing media partnerships and relationships to raise the social media profile of the campaign or organization. Determine interest and options to provide column, blog feed, commentary, and opinion to traditional and emerging news organizations through their own social media and online channels.

Build new media partnerships.

Approach rising efforts — mainstream, PACs, citizen groups, etc. — to negotiate content sharing agreements, including feeds, events, and conversations for their sites and audiences. Be an available resource to connect with their own followers. For example, if they invite you to participate in an online chat through their own social networks, do it.

Bring influential thought leaders to share commentary through the campaign online channels.

Host regular guest bloggers or video chats with thought leaders noted for alignment your campaign's mission, and have them share with their own followers and networks.

Step 9: Make sure you have contingency social media plans in place if — and when — the negative issues emerge.

Every campaign and organization should have a crisis communications playbook, and now is the time to update it to include social media considerations. A potential crisis is a potential crisis, and social media channels just make it grow faster. But the channels can resolve the crisis faster, as well. Make sure your staff has taken the time to create scenarios, such as "gotcha moments," and have a good plan in place for how to respond.

For example: Having someone from your staff immediately share the stinky diaper photo from the parade, as soon as it hits online, with a funny observation, can help diffuse the attempt to paint your candidacy as anti-family, as well as show your human side.

Step 10: Monitor and track against metrics that really show how much people "like" your campaign and take action on your behalf.

"Like." "Dislike." Remember, it's not about the rate at which the information moves, or how many social media channels exist, isn't what really matters. So don't just count posts, or comments, or retweets — the expression of voters is what truly matters. Explore the reach and influence of what you communicate through all channels (paid, earned, owned, and social). Endorse a targeted set of stronger measures that encompass the whole of your communication efforts.

Examples of measurement attributes that apply to social media:

- Share of voice
- Reach
- Prominence
- Tone (neutral, positive, negative)
- Endorsement
- Likelihood to support, fund, vote, endorse

These can blend well with polling, fundraising, and other campaign communications measures.

A variety of tools exist for adding social media to this measurement mix. Seek out the counsel of your communications staff for the best recommendations that fit into your current campaign measures. And make sure the results feed into your governing approach — or into your next campaign strategy.

Chapter 5
The Golden Rule in the age of LIKE

While the 10 steps outlined in this book will quickly set your campaign or organization on the path to true engagement with your constituents and stakeholders via social media, the rules take time and practice to learn. Give yourself and your staff some latitude as you go along the social media journey — and if you hit a snag along the way, go back to the rules, and you'll soon figure a way to move forward.

But if you take nothing else away from the rules of LIKE, never forget this:

Make sure you can stand behind or live up to anything you say or share on social media. If you can't, then don't say it.

This is not a permission slip to again ignore social media. It's a reminder that social media has made it possible for us to share everything, from anywhere, and everywhere, whenever we want. We can, and we do. But we are also human. Sometimes we fail to stop first, and ask ourselves if we should.

Some of the worst mistakes are made in social media because common sense is ignored. Former United States Representative Anthony Weiner's fall from grace in early 2011, thanks to his misuse of Twitter, is perhaps the most scathing of exhibits. Be clear on this reality: Once something is put out in the social media circles, it's virtually impossible to remove it.

And this is why the rules of LIKE are so critical for today's civic landscape. The conversation has permanently shifted. We need to consider the relationships and conversations with people we're trying to engage as never before. We need to realize they matter more to today than ever.

They will choose whether to like what you stand for and what you say. And you now have what you need to have the right conversations with them, and begin to earn their "likes."

Acknowledgments

The four of us met in 2010, during our year in the Policy Fellows program through the Hubert H. Humphrey School of Public Affairs, University of Minnesota. Together, we explored the gaps in social media use by candidates in the 2010 Minnesota gubernatorial race. Many individuals contributed time, experiences, perspectives and guidance to our research, which we presented in June 2011 at the conclusion of our year as Fellows. We would be horribly remiss if we did not take the opportunity to thank them here, as their collective wisdom helped guide our thinking and approach to the rules and steps contained in LIKE.

Together, we would like to thank:

The University of Minnesota Hubert H. Humphrey School of Public Affairs: Lawrence Jacobs, Walter F. and Joan Mondale chair for Political Studies and director of the Center for the Study of Politics and Governance; Kate Cimino, assistant director, Center for the Study of Politics and Governance; and all of the 2010-2011 Policy Fellows.

Jeff Blodgett, founding director of Wellstone Action, for presenting our Fellows cohort with a policy framework that has served as our compass.

The 2010 campaign staffs of Minnesota Governor Mark Dayton and Tom Emmer, for their candor during our group project research.

Tom Horner, for his candor regarding the 2010 gubernatorial race and his unwavering support and encouragement of our work.

Rick Mahn, Jackie Bateman, Jason DeRusha, Kevin Zimmerman, Greg Swan, Shannan Paul, Mike Keliher, Jon Austin, Joe Loveland, and Ted Davis, who served as our team of experts, tolerated our focus group questions and shared meaningful observations on social media, policy, and communications.

Nate Garvis, for additionally — and relentlessly — challenging us to stretch beyond our comfort zones.

Lars Leafblad, who single-handedly drove interest in our initial work to a level that kept the idea of this book alive.

Jocelyn Hale, executive director at the Loft Literary Center, for her encouragement and guidance.

Kelly additionally thanks Laura Bishop for her encouragement, plus her colleagues at Best Buy Co., Inc., who have inspired her with their smart, innovative uses of social media. Above all, she thanks Matt (Ole) and Jack Olson, her husband and son, for their unconditional love and support.

Dave thanks Maura, Ryan and Bailey, for understanding what it takes to be successful in any endeavor and being there when he needs them most.

Greg thanks Zach Rodvold and Dana Anderson, and sends special thanks to Martina Morgan for her love and support.

Bass thanks Zach Rodvold and Dana Anderson.

About the Authors

Kelly Groehler is a public relations strategist who advises multinational corporations and nonprofit organizations on strategic communications, reputation management, and stakeholder engagement. She specializes in positioning and storytelling for a variety of industry sectors and business trends, including sustainability, industrial supply chains and manufacturing, growth and innovation, labor relations, consumer retail, policy engagement, and women's issues. She also has built progressive models for sharing news, information and content through the use of consumer technology, including social media. Accredited in public relations, Kelly supports causes to help end domestic violence, ensure equality, and drive civic participation. She lives in Robbinsdale, Minn.

Dave Ladd is president of RDL & Associates, a strategic consulting firm that assists clients seeking solutions to issues that impact agriculture and the rural economy. He has a broad range of contacts at the federal, regional and state levels, and relationships with key leaders in production agriculture, the renewable energy sector, agribusiness, financial institutions, state and federal government and Capitol Hill. Dave is often sought for his expertise regarding agricultural and rural issues, and has served as a consultant to numerous state and federal candidates. A native of Hutchinson, Minn., he currently resides in Woodbury, Minn.

Greg Swanholm works for the United States Senate, focusing on military and veterans' issues. Additionally he's responsible for outreach to the organized labor community. A Senate staffer since 2007, Greg has handled a variety of areas for the Senate, from Medicare and Social Security to federal employee issues and the Bureau of Prisons. A native of Anoka, Minn., Greg is a graduate of the University of Minnesota and currently lives in South Minneapolis.

Bass Zanjani has worked in a broad range of policy advisory and communications roles for more than a decade. Currently the deputy district director for Congressman Keith Ellison, he formerly served as the first youth violence prevention coordinator for the City of Minneapolis, managing the city's "Blueprint for Action" initiative which has helped reduce youth violence rates. Bass is a former chief of staff at a North Minneapolis community health center, served as an aide to United States Senators Dianne Feinstein and the late Paul Wellstone, and has worked on human rights issues for the Baha'i International Community in Haifa, Israel. Bass holds an undergraduate degree from the University of Minnesota, where he is currently seeking a master's degree in public affairs.

www.ingramcontent.com/pod-product-compliance
Lightning Source LLC
Chambersburg PA
CBHW021938170526
45157CB00005B/2341